Sekiya Miyoshi

Jacob's Ladder

THE
PILGRIM
PRESS

Cleveland

A long time ago, twin baby boys were born in Israel. They did not get along. Even before they were born, they quarreled—kicking and tumbling. Their mother did not know what to do, so she prayed to God.

God gave a reply. "You will have two children with very different hearts. People will be bothered because of their constant quarrels."

God's message unsettled their mother, but the babies were born. The older was named Esau while the younger was named Jacob.

Esau and Jacob were very much alike. Indeed, they were exactly alike except for their hair. Esau had dark curly hair while Jacob had little hair.

As God had said, their hearts were different.
Esau liked to run, but Jacob liked to sit quietly.
Esau liked to hunt, but Jacob liked to cook.
Esau liked to track deer, but Jacob liked to set
the table.
Esau liked to eat big meals, but Jacob mostly
poked at his food.

Jacob thought that Esau was too bossy and noisy. One day Jacob shouted, "Esau, I don't want to live with you any more. You play too rough, and you do whatever you want. I'm going to find a quieter home."
With that, Jacob made a face and trotted toward the hills.

Jacob clambered up the hill. Then he climbed up the mountain. It was so quiet and peaceful. All he heard was his own footsteps. Even as the sun set beyond the desert, he was so glad to be away from Esau.

Finally Jacob was tired. He spotted a big stone for a pillow and a patch of smooth sand for a bed. He lay alone. Not a sound was heard. It was so quiet, so peaceful, and so lonely . . .

Jacob's big eyes were wet with tears. It was too quiet, too lonely. He watched the night sky above him.
Then, look!
Suddenly the sky opened up. A big hole appeared. From this hole a white thing came down. "It looks like, like what?" he wondered.

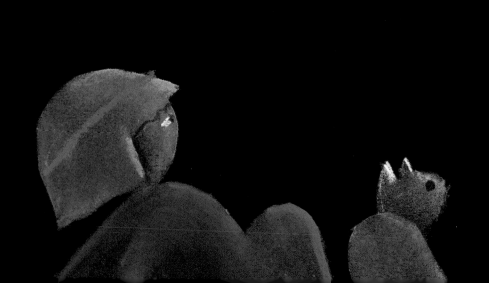

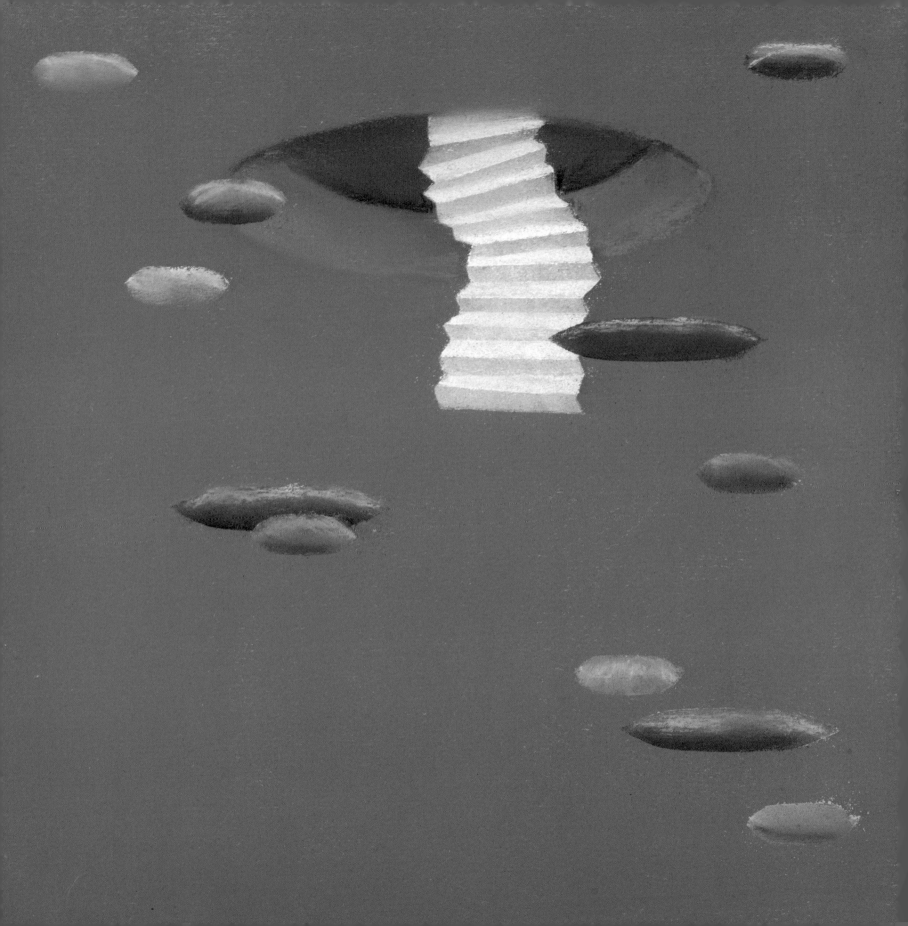

It kept coming down from the sky!
It was a staircase or a ladder.
It connected the sky above with
the earth below.

On this ladder between the sky and the ground,
little angels were playing together.
They climbed up and down. Some angels stood
while others sat. Some pushed their friends into
flight. Others tugged on their neighbors to
climb up and down with them.
"These little angels are having fun together,"
thought Jacob. "They are doing many different
things."

When morning came, Jacob decided
to mark the place where this ladder
had come down. "This is a gateway to
heaven," he thought. Such a gateway
should not be lost, and he might want
to come back here again.
So he placed many stones on his
stone pillow to make a big sign.

As he picked up stones, he found two that were exactly the same. "What's this?" he asked himself. "These stones are the same size, the same shape, the same weight. Only their colors are different."

"Stones do not fight," he murmured.
"They cannot move by themselves.
So they share and stare at each
other." Inspecting these twin stones,
it occurred to Jacob that they were
like he and his brother Esau.

"If these stones were far apart," he sighed, "they would be lonely." Jacob thought, "Maybe brother Esau is also lonely. I am alone. And he is alone."

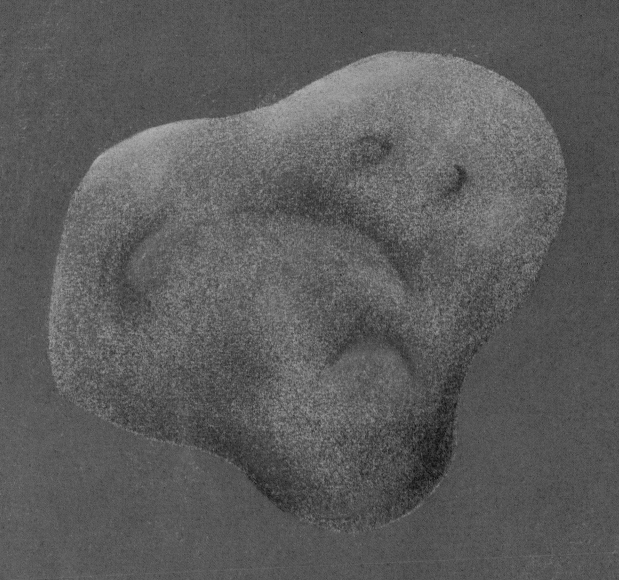

Suddenly, Jacob began to run.
He ran over the mountain, he
ran down the hill.
He ran as fast as he could.

In his hands were the two
stones of exactly the same
shape.

"Esau, Esau," he cried. "I'm back. I'm with you again. I don't want to be alone any longer. I've brought you presents—an Esau stone and a Jacob stone."

"Jacob, Jacob," Esau called back. "I missed you. I don't want to be alone, either. We are good brothers. We can be good friends. Let's each work and play in our own ways."

"It's no fun to be the same," Jacob said. "God's ladder has shown me how fun things can be when we are different."

"There are brown and gray deer," Esau said. "And black and white puppies." "There are singing and dancing angels," Jacob said. "And dark and light children."

"Yes," the brothers said together, "we will be together. We will play like the angels on God's ladder between earth and sky."

First published in North America 2001
by The Pilgrim Press
700 Prospect Aveue
Cleveland, Ohio 44115-1100 U.S.A.
pilgrimpress.com
Illustration and Original Text
Copyright © 1988 by Hisae Miyoshi
Original Japanese Edition "Yakobuto
Tenno Hashigo" published in 1988
by Shiko-Sha Co. Ltd., Tokyo, Japan
English text © 2001 The Pilgrim Press
Printed in China
06 05 04 03 02 01   1 2 3 4 5
ISBN 0-8298-1454-X